A Farmer's Chants

Poetry in Prose

Anwer Ghani

inner child press, ltd.

Credits

Author
Anwer Ghani

Editor
hülya n. yılmaz, Ph.D.

Cover Graphics & Design
William S. Peters Sr.

inner child press, ltd.

*In order to maintain a semblance of authenticity, certain texts embodying the unique aspects of the author's native tongue have not been edited.

General Information
A Farmer's Chants
Anwer Ghani

1st Edition: 2019

This Publishing is protected under the Copyright Law as a "Collection". All rights for all submissions are retained by the individual author and or artist. No part of this publishing may be reproduced, transferred in any manner without the prior **WRITTEN CONSENT** of the "Material Owner" or its representative, Inner Child Press International. Any such violation infringes upon the Creative and Intellectual Property of the Owner pursuant to International and Federal Copyright Law. Any queries pertaining to this "Collection" should be address to the Publisher of Record.

Publisher Information

Inner Child Press International:
www.innerchildpress.com

This Collection is protected under U.S. and International Copyright Laws.

Copyright © 2019: Anwer Ghani

ISBN-13: 978-1-970020-83-0 (inner child press, ltd.)

$ 10.95

Dedicated to

the glorious poet
Charles Simic

Table of Contents

xi　　　　　　　　　　　　　　　　*Preface*

The Poetry

3	Colorful Hearts
4	A Pale Land
5	The Old Castle
6	The Faint Light
7	Silvery Chants
8	A Farmer from the South
9	Dead Dreams
10	A Simple Man
11	Rainy Wishes
12	Birds
13	The Gypsy Girl
14	Cold Passion
15	The River-y Flowers
16	Fences
17	A Sad Shadow
18	A Dry Breeze
19	A Sandy Man
20	Southern Daughters
21	Pink Wishes
22	The Soul of Light
23	Windy Moments
24	Whispers
25	My Grandmother's Tales

Table of Contents ... *continued*

26	Red Winter
27	Valentine Birds
28	A Magical Veil
29	A Colorful Evening
30	The Red Cloak
31	The Blind Man
32	Secrets
33	Bizarre Souls
34	The Strange City
35	A Strange Holiday
36	The Door of Freedom
37	A Grey Winter
38	My Warm Silence
39	I Cannot Die as a Soldier
40	The Free Bird
41	Salty Remnants
42	Our Earth
43	A Grey Tale
44	Rocky Flowers
45	Mirrors
46	The Old Farmer
47	The Bare Land
48	The Pained Land
49	Glamorous Gardens
50	Summer Is Not Beautiful
51	Our Crazy Summer
52	The Faceless Land
53	A Thirsty Bean
54	The Dark Summer

Table of Contents ... *continued*

55	The River's Face
56	Al-Mehdi
57	The Arab River
58	A River's Tales
59	The Magical Wind
60	The Colorless City
61	The Blind Wind
62	The Blind City
63	Violet Tales
64	Nothing in My Soul but Loss
65	Dreamy Butterflies
66	Blind Hotels
67	Crying
68	Grey Butterflies
69	Spring's Lover
70	I Love Writers
71	A Bloody Lake
72	A Bitter Soul
73	He Who Saw Light
74	A Pale Man
75	The Grey Bird
76	The Silent Tree
77	The Glorious Friday
78	Illusions
79	The Cloud-Tales
80	A Remote Scent

Epilogue

83	about the Author

Preface

A realistic imagination and narrative imagery transpire as the foundation of the prose poems of *A Farmer's Chants*.

Poetry is a mirror, and the text is its vehicle; in its essential existence, the poetic text then is a large mirror. When we use prose to compose poetry, we create another mirror in actuality, and when we narrate our lyricism, we add an additional mirror to the entire process. Thus, narrative prose poetry represents a highly complex system of mirrors, and in every poetic moment there is a mirror. This book embodies a narrative-lyric writing with a narrative structure on the surface and an internal lyricism.

Everything in life aims to present itself in a fully trans-figurative state. Poetry too tries to self-present in full transfiguration. Freedom is of the essence for poetry and its total revelation.

In the world of prose poetry, we come across the phenomenon of anti-narrative narrative writing. For me, the prose poem is a poetic text that is written as one horizontally shaped extension which depends on anti-narrative narrative writing as well as an abstract imaginary disclosure.

In literature, there is poetry, prose, and in the middle, prose poetry, as identified according to the characteristics of the surface and structural elements of language. Every speech or its written form has a surface makeup which constitutes a basic structure, enabling our aural or visual perception, and a multifaceted structure which transforms our understanding to an analytic and semantic level. Poetry is distinguished by rhythmic surface and comprehensive structures. Prose on the contrary is characterized by unrhythmic external and multilayered structures. In prose poetry, then, we find the unrhythmic outward structure *and* the rhythmic internal one. It is these aspects through which this particular genre brings the concept of hybridity into the field of literature. In sum, prose poetry is a combination of prose and poetry *and* rhythmicity and non-rhythmicity.

Prose poetry can be produced in a narrative or lyric manner. If the style is lyric on both surface and analytical levels, the outcome would be lyric prose poetry. If the style is narrative on those same levels, the literary product will be narrative prose poetry. However, the surface narrative structure can also be found within the analytical lyric structure. In this case, a hybrid genre will come about; namely, a narrato-lyric prose poetry, and as such, it will be the embodiment of a second hybrid inside the first hybrid of proso-poetry. Hence, in the context of narrato-lyric prose poetry, this book represents a hybrid inside a hybrid.

The poems in this collection have been written between 2016 and 2018, and the cornerstone of their themes encompasses two conceptualizations: The impact of war on the soul and the glorification of an unassuming life.

It may be said that *A Farmer's Chants* is an imaginary narrative of war's darkness and a realistic praise of simplicity.

Anwer Ghani

A Farmer's Chants

Poetry in Prose

Anwer Ghani

Anwer Ghani

A Farmer's Chants

Colorful Hearts

The hearts of birds are so hidden that I cannot see them well. Sometimes I decide to open my sorcerous wooden box to see the exact color of these runaway hearts. They are very old. When you turn their leaves, the scents of old southern adventures will rise. No moon can sit around these colorful hearts because their brilliant rays will blind even the daring eyes of the sun.

There are no clear roads in the horizon . . . just a wide space and its infinite moments which will amaze your heart. I feel it – this amazement penetrating us as an old tale. On its hand, we find all the colorful souls which put eternal kisses on our lips. Their hands rain astonishment over our heads, and their smiles plant colorful roses in our surroundings. Please touch them gently! They are as delicate as a shy girl's dream.

When we see these multi-hued shadows, their whispers penetrate us fast, and when we smell the fragrance of their revelations, the sun sleeps in our dreams as a blue butterfly. In a matchless moment – an absent moment, all the warm letters and deep ecstasies dissolve in us as sugar. That is . . . when we touch these shadows and hear their colorful wishes.

Anwer Ghani

A Pale Land

This is what I see, what I feel and what my moments tell me. I am from here, from this earth, the designated pallor. There is no moon here and no lovers . . . there is nothing here, just pale tears. I will go deeply into pain's tales. I will hide from living eyes because I am just a pale remnant.

Please touch me, but touch me softly because I am a pale relic. My mouth is full with absence, and my heart is filled with illusion. Please touch me! I want to feel my self and to know that I am a pale soul, . . . a common soul. Here in my land, everything is pale and hides even me. Here in my land, the land of pale tears, everything is sad. Even the sun.

Blood colors our brooks with its redness, but it leaves our faces utterly pale. I am from the pale land where you cannot see colorful flowers and cannot hear melodic birds. Look at our boys! They are pale. Look at our girls! They are pale. The trees here are pale, the rivers are pale and hearts are pale. Our lips are pale, our hands are pale and our eyes are pale. In fact, we are just pale vestiges.

A Farmer's Chants

The Old Castle

We have an old castle we inherited from our ancestors. Its façade is grey, and its rivers are very short. They had made its legs from clipped bamboo and its head from rumbling tales. But when you open its bone, you will find just a time-worn paper. When we try to kiss its mouth, there is nothing but illusions.

Yes, I know that you have high castles. I need strong eyes to see their ornaments inside, but their trees know very well that the lovely wells are thirsty, and their pale leaves fall on my head with sad stories. Yes, I know that I have a very old castle which vaporizes every night with smooth winds. My grandfather said that those winds come from the high castle.

Yes, our hands are so coarse and our trees so brown that there is nothing in our hearts but blustery tales. Our eyes can see the sunset with its amazing colors when it sleeps near our castle. You should take a step to see our magic afternoons and to hear the incredibly melodic chants of our birds. Despite our sad rivers, we do not attempt to plant tears in your fields, and despite our love for an ease, we do not try to eat your ivory castles.

Anwer Ghani

The Faint Light

When my eyes see that faint light, hidden thoughts dance with strange shadows deep inside, asking about that light which penetrates my silence thoroughly. You may want to see my soul jumping over the grass with these shadows; you may like to know how this faint light embodies my dreams, my thoughts and my truth. You might not know that you are that faint light.

I am a farmer from the south where there is no light or moon. My skin is a swaying goose and my eyes are dawn's waiter. But, in a hidden night, where our birds were sleepy and my father's ship had immersed deeply in its dream, I saw a dancing light in our orchard. We have no light, but that dancing light visited us in an absent night.

A Farmer's Chants

Silvery Chants

I am nothing but a boat. Its wing has silvery chants. I cannot tell you their secrets. When the silvery voice first showed me its soul, mysterious whispers dissolved in my dream as a sleepy rose. I can tell you about another mystical glance. There are silvery seas, and you can feel their fingers touch you inside with a calm wonder. No, I am not a sorcerer. I am just a passenger who cannot sit still when my talk is about lively horses. There were cities of silver. Its whispers touched our windows with smiles, penetrated our souls without delay and invaded them with a genuine salute. I was a mere young child. You cannot expect to find any fairies in my pockets, but our land is the daughter of a silvery voice. Yes, I was just a charming child of the south, sitting on a tree branch, with silvery chants in his small pockets.

Anwer Ghani

A Farmer from the South

I am a farmer from the south, bringing along nothing in his pockets but oranges. Look at my face, it is brown. Look at my hands, they are white. I am from here, from the south, an eastern man with a dreamy soul. Yes, I am a dreamer from the south. My heart bears nothing but simple love, and my mouth smiles without a reason.

I am an old farmer who knows the amazing colors of flowers' hearts where blue dreams wear their shiny dresses and whispers make a sunny cake for the birds of the morning. When the squirrel travels through green songs, all flavors wear their pink veils, and when the rivers chant their daring stories, every girl immerses in her blue dreams. Those dreams fill time with a stormy passion and plant smiles in our dry deserts. In their sleepy eyes, you can see the river's secrets, and in their loud whispers, you may recognize the silent wishes.

A Farmer's Chants

Dead Dreams

My grandfather had a ship, but I think he could not imagine the size of my dream. I mean . . . my motionless dream. I also have a ship, but I have no wings and no feet. Here in my chest, there is nothing but crippled wishes. I mean . . . beautiful wishes, but there are no roads nor trains. In other words, I am a lifeless man immersed in this useless dream. Please look at me! Do you see our dry sea? Look at our ship! It is just an illusion. Yes, it is just a ship of dead dreams.

I am so sad that my soul is useless and my life is a bag of dreams. My legs are crippled and my arms are very short. Oh, great world, please give me a wing! Just a single small wing that I may see the windows below. No, I am not an underground creature, but there is no sun, no moon here, and we live our days blindly and quietly. Yes, we are out of date. But we, as you, have dreams, and we, as you, have wishes.

Anwer Ghani

A Simple Man

I am a simple man from the south where green dreams color the sun's eyelashes. My smile is faint, but my eyes are bright; so, I can travel through infinity as a shadow. I see a light now; it is as silvery and soft as the moon. I see a brave ship swimming in my destroyed ocean. It is flying in my illusions with the tales of birds. Yes, I am here, inside this motionless body – a young eastern man who drowns in his shameful hesitance.

Dark sands hide my butterflies behind the illusions and distribute roses of death on the roads. They are blind like our sunset which has no face. It leaves me alone in the cold night-tales, but from the dry air, I will make my milk and from its bronze breath, I will make a river. Yes, I am the son of sand sitting on top of the hill, repeating old songs. I am a grey body and know nothing about the sun. It is I, the simple man who was growing up in a dry desert. My dreams travel with the evening like migratory birds, and my life is as negligible as that of a cat under heavy rain.

I am living in a faceless desert. You cannot see the junctions of my heart, and all that I can imagine is my grey tree branch. We should be good and laughing exactly like my grandfather, but I am a simple man who knows nothing about the grass. This earth, which I will always love, stands over my shoulder with cold extremities. So, I cannot see her gloomy face, while I touch everything in her abode.

A Farmer's Chants

Rainy Wishes

The face of Earth will be grim without the childish jumping of the raindrops. Yes, rain is a pleasant diversion which had planted ambergris in the hearts of our farmers. My ancestors have taught their souls the wisdom of dreadful waiting, and kneaded their mud with its tales; so, you may see them sitting in their narrow gardens with rainy wishes. They look at the sky and whisper with yearning. Yes, you are right. I am the inheritor of silence and rainy wishes.

Rain is the tear of yearning. I remember when the sky had ascended toward its throne; she kept looking at her sister, Earth, with deep passion. Silently, she was sending kisses with the wind's wings, but when yearning grew, her eyes teared with rain. Yes, the raindrops are the grieving tears of a transparent soul.

I like the rain because it is the portrayal of love. His color is wet but warm, and his hand is cold but kind. He comes in the evening as an old tale and hugs small leaves with passion. When we get lost in our rainy moments, we find a breeze embracing our bare souls. I cannot imagine how miserable I would feel, if I could not see raindrops dance.

Anwer Ghani

Birds

Here on earth, birds are brown, and their hearts are delicate like women. You can see our palm trees; they are pretty, and you can see our birds; they are wise like the builders of Uruk. Obscure strangers had tried to steal my grandmother's colorful carpet, but our amazing birds have unwound their magic and negated their wicked amulets.

I am so happy because our earth has a colorful dress and her birds are still deeply in love with her despite all these dark nights of war. Our birds are neither lame nor ugly, but the dark wind is harsh and a liar. I always stand under that tree, and when the sun opens her eyes, I see how our birds kiss the smiling earth passionately.

Our birds are very smart singers. In the morning, they teach me warm passion, and they plant in my soul the calm of peace in the evening. What a lucky man I am! With these true avian storytellers, I can cross the magical oceans and hear the hidden desires of faraway fairies. I am not a romance narrator, but I want to tell you that our earth is still beautiful and our birds are still lovers.

A Farmer's Chants

The Gypsy Girl

I like our quiet lakes and their revitalizing breeze, where water's eyes are always sleepy. You cannot imagine the ruddy face of winter nights. I remember when my mother made a nice hat for it. My mother is an expert in the souls of seasons. She told me that autumn is a gypsy girl. I have never seen autumn, but I am sure that my mother saw her because she described her features precisely. She told me that autumn flies between tree branches as a small bird and weaves her veil cheerfully in our souls. Sometimes I feel that autumn is a fairy and you may see her stormy tale swimming deeply in our dreams' water. My grandfather is also an expert in seasons' souls. He had a beautiful horse and was filled with compassion toward her. I did not see her, but they said that she was legendarily brave. My family might have possessed a carriage. I do not know and I did not ask about this. But I think, if we had one, it will be sealed like the desert's souls. I am a man of Arabia, and you know there is nothing here but desert. So, I have decided to bring a gypsy wagon to my home to teach my children the freedom and some of the tales about the gypsy girl.

Anwer Ghani

Cold Passion

It has stolen any possible warmth from the basket of my days; so, I was delightedly standing under that tree as a drenched bird. This lovely coldness intentionally cut my skin with her hidden knife, and destroyed my face like the water of a frozen lake. She had fiercely slapped me; so, you now see the redness on me every morning.

I am a man of the twenty-first century, and my legs had dipped in the soul of the earth as an old cow. I do not like the darkness or its cold voice, but my hand was frozen like a woman's coat, and my friends' hearts were hung on the absent trees of our coldness.

Our sun has a thick veil, and many daughters are with heavy hearts; they are lightless and cold. Everything under our cold sun is icy and soundless, even our evenings which were travelling among ambergrises as blind grasshoppers. They are like an eternal hero eating up all the beauty and building all the glory on our backs. Please, do not ask me about their skirts or hair, because in addition to my blindness, they have cloudy faces, and we only know that they arrived here through their cold winds.

A Farmer's Chants

The River-y Flowers

When the morning starts his journey, and the squirrel travels through his green songs, all the flavors take their azure veils. Flowers, women, and old farmers know the amazing colors of the river-tales where blue dreams wear light dresses, and faint whispers make an aurorean cake from dawn's early smiles. Time is an absent moment without the river-y passion, and places are just dry deserts without colors. Through their hidden secrets, we see our sleepy dreams, and from their loud wishes, we write poetry with hidden letters.

The blue flowers of our river see the womanly glances that teach the world its marvelous existence and give life to its shining love. When days try to sing their beauty, they will intonate their magic chants, and when the rainbow decides to wear its colors, it will take from their beautiful cloaks. Yes, magical lands see their wonderful smiles on the face of our river-flowers, and winds cannot find their earrings without mirrors. The river-y wind is a legendary tale penetrating our soul with her stormy love. It colors our world with its unique zest, gives life its spicy taste, and its glances teach hearts their yearning. The river is our wavy essence, and the wind is a free woman under an orange-hued shroud.

Anwer Ghani

Fences

The fish are pure and a real water-lover; so, they will promptly die without its kisses. The fish, unlike I, know nothing but the truth, and do anything to live freely. When blindness puts barriers on the river's chest, I hear the voice of a fish, and I see the blood. The barriers are a face of death, absence and theft, but when you look at my hands, you may know that I am a smashed dam. I am neither a horse nor a rabbit. When the sunset kisses their old thicket, I realize the sweetness of a fence-less life, but when all these horses with their heroes stand on my back, I remember our war's children. You know, the grass is green and horses are beautiful, but who will love my little rabbit? Because of this, I will die alone in a dark soul, away from your solid fences and bitter allusions. I will live in a horse's forehead, behind the lovely fences. I mean . . . beyond any fervor. Yes, I remember my grandmother's white cloth which she used to make cheese in. In fact, I had liked that cloth because I did not like milk and because it was real and white. But you see, our days' dams are red and gloomy. They, like my heart, are bitter and dark, and their hands are filled with lies.

A Farmer's Chants

A Sad Shadow

I am a dry leaf from Iraq. I know nothing about beauty or artists. All that I know is the blood and tales of war. Here in my broken chest resides a faint boy who lives on this vast earth with a small soul and walks through it with his hidden face. My trees are grey and my dreams are sad shadows. When I open my twilight, I hear our weeping birds. When I close down my evening, I see our slain moon.

I am an Iraqi man, and my soul has been kneaded with the tales of war. Our streets, which are immersed in war's scent, roam in the desert of sadness, and like our girls, they always dream of fire-free days. We are here, under clouds of worry, waiting for migrant holidays, but our legs inherited gloomy faces. Here on my crying earth, there is no rose, and you cannot see anything else but sad rivers. Here in my city, you will find a rough moon which is the son of our caudex.

Anwer Ghani

A Dry Breeze

With its breeze, the evening has planted in my soul unforgettable tales. I do not like the crying, and as any man, I wish to fall deeply in love, but with my chopped-up tress and my lonely streets, I am a man from the ruined land. My dreams were killed like those of a beautiful bird, and my smile was stolen on a bright day. I am standing under that dry tree as a shadow without feet or a head. I try to cry, and always attempt to wash off my bitter heart, but the stormy wind is constantly coloring my soul with a dry breeze. It is as delicate as a green apple. Under its wings, towns live in stillness, and swans dance like the sun's songs. The field-birds, with their vivid colors, bathe over its swings with delight. Wet leaves fill the streets with morning songs and soak girls' hearts with dreams. It comes from a remote land on the wings of softness. Its sleepy eyelashes color my blue dreams with the taste of a pearl. They are bashful, but they inspire my body into an unforgettable heartbeat. They hit my head with their stones; so, I feel incompetent. In their hands, the gentle Saba-breeze appears more peaceful. How can I touch their tales?

A Farmer's Chants

A Sandy Man

I feel your soul and I can grasp all the romantic night-stars, but I cannot love you because I am a sandy man who knows nothing but dryness. Yes, I hear your voice and I can see your face, but I cannot love you because I am a sandy man who bears nothing but sadness. Believe me, I have immersed in every awesome, unexpected moment, and I can smell the essence of the sea flowers, but I cannot love you because I am just a war-remnant that has no heart.

My times are always alone, and my birds are always pale. All my nights shiver, and all my fish are mute, but in the midst of this coldness, I can hear the ocean, and his soul colors my heart with a lovely blue warmness.

I am from the south. My skin is brown and it turns darker whenever I hear about the giant salmon of Japan. I have an amazing coffee that colors my days, but the story does not start with my grandfather's coffee beans; for, my coffee is of the instant kind. I will tell you a secret now: I am a farmer, and I take delight in vanishing in our coffee's flavor so that you may see the brown veils covering my face. But be careful, do not touch me because I am a sandy man.

Anwer Ghani

Southern Daughters

I am from the south where trees are dry and rivers are waterless. Our sky is dark and our sun is foggy. I am from that south where everything is colorless. The fields have daughters but the streets are always blind. These daughters are always smiling with eyes tormented by hidden tears. Their hearts are sad, and their dreams have broken wings. Our southern daughters are miracles, and their braids give the sea its luminous blueness. They are secret daughters of the sea living in the fields as butterflies. Their colorful wings bring delightful waters from a distant well, and their breaths make me swim in a faraway lake. They are beautiful, peculiar and intense, but hidden. Their glowing faces have been covered by a dark veil and their soft hearts have been smashed by my primitiveness. Yes, they are the secret springs' daughters; their wings make me swim in a secluded sea. You may see their summer, but you need a butterfly's heart to touch their glowing faces.

A Farmer's Chants

Pink Wishes

Here in my land, you can see everything, but be careful because our wells are pink and dreamy. Here in my land, you may find me on that tree limb with a pink face and a pink voice, but be careful because the wind here is also pink. Here in my heart, you will find yourself, but be careful because your pink wishes will disappear very fast.

I am a farmer from the desert. Look at my old cloak and you will know the story. Yes, there may be hidden wishes in my heart, but believe me there is nothing else here . . . just pink wishes. In an absent morning, I feel dreamy and I see the phantoms of these wishes. Yes, foliage can occur in the desert as an absent dream. Just believe me. I am the farmer from a green desert.

Anwer Ghani

The Soul of Light

When the roads open their eyes, all the blue fish come to my sea. The road is a smile that exits its pink ear from that window which sleeps on my mother's hand. Without any delay, I am disappearing in its light where the warmness wears its white coat. My heart, like a bird on an icy tree branch, will immerse in that moment which comes from her chant . . . the soul of light. My love is that wind which can bring all the clouds of the sky and that grass which hugs all the goats of the world, but a mother's love is a different world and impossible in its oneness.

When the morning's happiness pours and the foggy shadow removes itself, I know that the sun has a pure, splendid face, and the wings of light laugh heartily. When the mask of darkness falls, I will see all the towers and the glorious rain chants on your hands where the secret springs of the universe have been immersed in the dust of clayish towns, misted by their brown breeze. I will see your azure trees smiling at the waterfalls and your carnelians submerging in the ice-tobacco of the Mashu Mountain. The white wings of your blooming spirit tell the earth tales of light which had been colored by a shawl of a girl who was gathering dates from her grandfather's orchard. Earth's mightiness bows in awe of your ancient glitter and flies as a space vehicle that has seen a new face of the moon.

A Farmer's Chants

Windy Moments

In our turbulent boat, you can see all the blue colors and the secret lands of dreams. When you reach those distant lands and see my pain, please ignite a candle in our cold night, and let this sleepy world know about the truthful light.

I know, you cannot remember the souls of flowers which have known nothing but beauty. But, when you drown deeply in our dreams and meet all the possible illuminations, you may find the bracing fingers of the poet. Through them, we have crossed the seas of sound where magical fields were singing their ballads. In those gleeful moments, some secret souls greeted us warmly, and as dazzled butterflies, we fell in love with Earth and exited from its crevices with the crown of our arduous years.

Anwer Ghani

Whispers

Do you know anything about the sea's whispers? Do you see the smiles which reside behind his veil? The sunset loves the sea, where the sun combs the hair of the fish and smoothly draws seasons on his tales. I have heard his whispers; they are filled with truth. I saw his dream in a precious moment. It was blue and magnificent.

It whispered from there: Where will you find your story? The violet roses are sleepy, and the mirrors follow the white trees. The birds and the fabled river know that moment which needs a smile and warmth.

It then said: The river's colors descend from that balcony and they kiss the eyes of the flower-seller.

It whispered further: When the moon sleeps on your eyelids, you will know a new kiss and you will see the cloud's flowers. I will drown in the yearning sea. I will hug that train where we meet sleepy sounds, and from there, my story will begin.

A Farmer's Chants

My Grandmother's Tales

I love the moon because his smile is bright like the tales of my grandmother. She used to whisper every night into my dream's ear, telling me the story of colorful birds in that faraway land. She was a good storyteller, and sometimes her tales surpassed our narrative poetry. I saw her ocean and sat beside its shore in that warm world. I told her my story and informed her about my cold years, of which grey souls had eaten away the shells. I told her that I did not like crying, but you see, there was no place for my smile. Those bloody souls had stolen my life. They said the body is the cause of sadness, but I found no truth in their red voices. I had heard my grandmother's tales as she whispered to my core being that the love of the moon did not need blood.

Anwer Ghani

Red Winter

You sit there, on that tree branch with my dream, but I cannot see your beauty because my eyes are drowning in the redness of the winter. I am a red man from the red land; my coat is worn-out, and my soul is shattered. There is no summer here and no spring flowers . . . just a red winter.

Our trees moan in red; so you see a red voice rising from their overwhelming remains. They are trying to come back from their isolation. They try to inhale the ardor of love, but a crazy fire colors them with red nectar. Yes, the desert-air is so dry and there are so many red plants and red animals that there is nothing here but redness and only shadows of lives. The water is red here, the air is red and the love-rose is red.

A Farmer's Chants

Valentine Birds

I am not a tree, and I cannot sleep in the hearts of these fountains, but lovers have made a home for Valentine-birds which know nothing else but love and utter nothing else but chants. They are the creatures of light. All the beginnings started from their journeys, and you can see chants laden with inner peace on their hands. Those Valentine-birds stand under love's trees and give me an amazing kiss, but my days, like my poems, are grey and tasteless, and they oftentimes ask me to throw them from that old bridge.

Yes, I am an old lover who cannot drink his coffee without shedding fiery tears, and whose heart has fiercely disappeared in distant cities where souls cannot speak anything else but love.

Yes, I will bring a jar of Valentine-smiles back from those cities to color my grey days. I will tell my land, love is a colorful treasure that I saw before the wedding of the Sun and the growth of the grass; so, our earth will wear a white dress, our shy whispers will breathe kindhearted gazes, and our birds will sing their chants.

Anwer Ghani

A Magical Veil

My palm tree is as beautiful as Abigail. Her eyelashes are as long as a river, and her veil came with the ancestors' souls to release our grim dreams. I can feel her curvy pulse and I can see her priceless appeal behind the shawl. Near her foot, there is a spring of magical water, and beside her wishes, I see my face which had been stolen as a yellow bird.

Yes, we have a thick curtain which is unintentionally masked by our pale moments, and she, without delay, arrives in the evening with foreign winds to comb our ragged hair. In fact, I cannot differentiate her from the faces of our days, and because of this confusion, sometimes I think that she is my mother. She stands there to lessen the voice of the light and to magnify our internal awareness, but because of its redness, she always remembers the sad stories of our stolen lives and the shameless manifestations of war.

A Farmer's Chants

A Colorful Evening

Our dreams have a colorful evening, which refreshes the hearts as a smiling girl. We like its whispers, but when its letters take real shapes there is nothing else but sadness. We, as blind trees, know nothing about its breeze. All that we know is a constant struggle to live and a continuous attempt to catch the remnants of this world. Our hands are as hot as the soul of the sunset. They have burnt our hearts with its passion; so, you cannot see anything else here but flowers. It comes with its reviving breeze to open our doors, but I am the blind son who knows nothing about its amazing orange hue. It fills my lungs with rebels' breaths and vanishes my dreams in freedom's wings. I have emerged from the weavings of its dress as a butterfly and disappeared in its red colors as a distant land.

Anwer Ghani

The Red Cloak

Life sits on her high chair and looks at me with a hidden smile. She knows that war had stolen our rainbow, and left me as bare as a rock. Yes, I am a grey man. I know nothing about vivid fragrances, and my dreams are faded like an old wood. Do you see these crevasses on our earth? They are our girls' hearts. They need water. Everything will be velvety when our thirsty souls find the water of peace.

My cloak was red. I am the son of wars, and all that you can see are my crippled remains. I do not remember anything about peaceful dresses, because our town's brides were killed before their weddings, and our land's face was smashed by the unknown. Now, we are loveless and know nothing about the moon's tales. We are always looking for our lost dresses in this large white world. Here, we cannot see our hands because they disappear in the mouth of war, and we cannot hear our voices because they drown in its absent ocean.

A Farmer's Chants

The Blind Man

Here in my crying earth, there is nothing else but pale faces and the rhyme of red pain. My eyes see nothing else but the empty sea, and I can feel the rocky hands of the world destroying my doors. Oh, you blind world, I cannot see your heart! I remember the time when you told me about your colorful trees. When you lay your head on their trunks, you should remember our children and their blood in your streams. Your blind winds have seen all the beauties on riverbanks; so, they cannot understand the cause of the salty blood in our water. They can see our pond, but there are no beavers in it because these salty souls push them away as if they were some outlandish butterflies. You told me about their magical marvel, but believe me, I cannot see anything else but a blind wind destroying my dreams. It is a memory that comes from faraway lands, telling us about the adventures situated deeply in our midst. It always tells me that the wind is a foreign leaf misleading us with illusions, but when we sleep, we see its face clearly. At that moment, it shows us its cold stories.

I am not a delusive mirror, but I feel that I am a colorful shadow, seeking a unique flower. When I find her, she will say: "Oh, seeker, sometimes you need to be blind to see clearly." I hear her voice, and see her face in my heart because I am a blind man.

Anwer Ghani

Secrets

When the sleepy leaves saw my red birds, I dissolved madly in the silent voices. Please, behold my shelved life! It is the beauty of my wasted love. Yes, I am yet embryonic; so, you see, my words wander freely and insanely. I am a sun-tanned man, not a blurred vision. I can count my fingers easily because I am as tiny as the delicacies my mother used to prepare. I am from here; from the south. I am always disappearing in our fountains' secrets. Please, look at our faces! When you see our eyes, you will find that our secrets are actually non-secret, and all those astonishing tales will reach your heart before the morning paean. Look at our earth! We are the farmers from the south; our dreams sleep before the columbine and our muteness protrudes from this land's furrows as shadows which know nothing about the secrets of eternal love.

Yes, it is I; a farmer from the south. My hair is grassy and my dream is heavy like an old train. If you touch my heart, you will see stream-like secrets, and if you open my chest, you will find colorful stones.

Yes, I can escort the sunset and catch its red roses, but I know nothing about their chants. Now, I will tell you a secret: don't love a farmer! For his feelings are embryonic yet, and his passion is volcanic all the time.

A Farmer's Chants

Bizarre Souls

Life is so vacant without the salt of infant souls. They color our rocky hearts with their frivolity and give small hares their flying winds. If your old trees had taught you the antique aloofness, you should discover your baby-like spring's warmness. I am not a delusional man but I know that the unusual souls are the blood of our world.

I feel their warm colors and unwind them in my dreams. Their voices are silvery like hidden waterfalls and their palms are smooth like enchanting moons. You can see the sunset in their eyes while they chant lucent songs. The surroundings are colored by their brown shadows, and barefoot boys jump over their grass as squirrels and fill their winds with faint smiles. It is so amazing to see smiles in my earth, the land of rare souls.

Anwer Ghani

The Strange City

We live in our earth under the wings of Azzalan. It was my grandfather's river, where he had trenched it in a heated moment; so, our souls were filled with warm songs. Despite all this purity of my skin, I am like any Iraqi youth turning my eyes toward the anonymous city. I want to die modestly and live in humiliation in that astonishing city which fills my heart with a colorful loneliness and a razor-sharp coldness.

A Farmer's Chants

A Strange Holiday

A holiday is a very delicate thing. We learned it in our childhood, as we learned to carry our bags. It is smooth as a summer-dream, filling our chests with spring-butterflies. I was very happy when I touched its heart. Its waterfalls amazed me. They were calm as the braids of girls. We saw that holiday and felt its sleepy hands. I saw clearly when it planted misty tales. That holiday, which came from a faraway town, stood with its silky coat in the middle of the street as a stranger. It dissolved in our veins as a letter of passion. I was very wrong when I assumed it to be a migrant goose.

Anwer Ghani

The Door of Freedom

I will vanish in love of the Euphrates like a slippery fish. I will learn the red chant so that the free land can smile for its lovers. It is my beginning toward the warm skies and my story in a waterfall where I kiss the foreheads of those who pass by. From there, the spikes of wheat will radiate in thousand lights and fill earth's lungs with the new dawn. Souls will be barren – no red tears . . . Listen to Husain's voice, look at the wide-open door of freedom! Look at the sadness of eternity, and softly grab its bashful bracelet . . . the space of the hopeful sun. He is the freedom's kiss. I will dissolve in its love without delay. He is Euphrates' true saying and a story which does not know any dreamy song. Listen to his scream: "There should be a new dawn to save this world from drowning."

A Farmer's Chants

A Grey Winter

Winter is a cruel knife that cuts my joints with cold blood. He is not smiling; he is grey just like my dream. This winter, which I feel vigorously, is not kind, and you can see the sad tears in its pocket. His rain colors my soul with pale smiles, and his harsh whisper plants unforgettable tales in the depths of my memory.

In grey winters, birds do not shiver because of love; they just shake their feathers, enjoying winter's stories. Here, winter dresses itself in a different color and a different cruelty, and all that can I see are pale shadows. Here, winter is not tender-hearted; in my grandfather's gloomy field, beans sway over the grass like a sad bride.

I am the son of winter; my ancestors left me alone in this frosted lake. Look at my face; it is colorless; feel my hands; they are short and dead.

The pain is deep in grey winters, and the smiles have left our garden without a goodbye. In its nights, I am just a shadow over the cold trees, and in its days, I am a blind owl.

This winter is blind and dry. There is nothing here but cold smiles and white dead flowers. Believe me, I have tried to plant a pink rose but the hands of this blind winter froze my heart. Its grey shroud knows the roads of my mute lips and the chill of my faceless moon.

Anwer Ghani

My Warm Silence

Can you hear my warm silence? Can you touch all that warmth? You are there, in that distant place seeing my cold veil. It covers my passionate yearnings with a frigid smile and colors my torrid wings with cold feathers. Can you feel them?

The winter's chants leave unforgotten memories in my streets. Their chilling moments are filled with silence. They freeze me like an old forest tree. The wretched ships vomit eternal pain, and the snowy trains penetrate my ears. They hide me in this vast space as an unexpected end and drown me in the mist; so, my words drop into the slime and my flowers run away.

On a cold night, my being has lost its eardrums. The pain was immense, and smiles left our garden like a Hoopoe. At that time, I was a shadow among the trees of faraway owls. They are strange, dry and blind. But there are also smiles and white flowers. I had tried to bring in a flower but that cold night was thick, red and its heart had a grey cloak. I think you will now know the causes of the motionlessness of our mute lips and the chilling cold of our faceless space.

A Farmer's Chants

I Cannot Die as a Soldier

My heart stumbles between valleys. Its feet are made of bitter ice and its eyes are remnants of a brassy sound. I had searched for a long time; I searched in every place where my fingers could reach. I searched in my grey color, and I searched in my ancestry, but I did not find a picture of a soldier. I know that I am impure and blind, but I should find my pureness in order to see the picture of that soldier who longs for free death. I am now so sad because I cannot die as a soldier, and I know that life has a smile which cannot be seen but by a soldier's death. I am standing here every day as a strange bird; I am standing here lonely and listening to that voice; my heart's voice. Yes, I am standing here every day, awaiting a return of my pure soul . . . to die as a soldier.

Anwer Ghani

The Free Bird

I am an old farmer who could not see his own reflection anywhere else but on the water's face. It was small like my dream. At that time, I had been a child dissolved in butterfly colors. Oh, the purity which they steal! They take our silky olives, make a missile from them, and then tell me that I am a dangerous plant.

Yes, without tiring, I shall repeat the birds' songs; I should not care about the world's brassy face, nor about the one-eyed city. Yes, I shall learn the earth, the rose's voice, and lonely winds will not find a place on my skin. I am a free bird loving the mud's scent, and because my father planted me with our wheat, I like the noon sun when it touches my face. You can feel my pulse with its great tales of the blind sand where echoes groan as a yellow bird, exhausted by the rain. It narrates its sharp pain with wide-open eyes. The crying clouds are ashamed because they dissolve its feathers and bring an autumn-roar, filled with a yearning death. Oh, the bitter yearning! I am not happy and cannot tell you my fiery passion, but you should remember that yellow bird and its grey blood.

A Farmer's Chants

Salty Remnants

After all that warmness which overflowed me with falls of light, I find myself just a crippled shadow. Here is my heart, look at it! Do you see anything except salt? I am the corpse which had been stormed by a deaf fever. I lean down on barefooted roads as a stranger, nothing recognizes me but the cold. In my salty soul, I cannot see anything else but groans. This is I: A salt-filled shadow dreaming of water-filled hands.

I am the son of war; I know nothing but smoke and see nothing but the color black. My rivers are filled with salty tears, and my dead children lie on dry streets like common rocks. Look at my hands; they were smashed like western papers, and look at my face which was stolen under a bright sun. I do not want any song or any celebration. All my wishes are so that I can see my women without weeping and hear my birds' chants without crying. O, you blind world, that which was killing my dreams in cold blood! O, humanity, that which had forgotten me like an extinct creature! I am a man from Iraq. Do you see me?

I am just a heap of salty remnants. Their ghosts ride on me like on a blind horse; so, I am good only for a clash with my trees. I do not see all that glory, but I can see a stone cutting my feet and a grim tree branch slashing my head.

Our Earth

The colors of our trees tell you the story. This earth is our heritage, and with no delay, we have disappeared in her fragrance. We are swimming in her lakes as fish and drown in her smiles as a sunset. Our earth has lucent wings and her birds wear white coats. So . . . you can imagine her beauty.

Our days are mirrors of our souls, and their smiles are chants of love. The night's kisses are just echoes of the morning roses. They turn white when the birds of our hearts are light, and they become grey when our dreams are heavy. They may show you our laughter or our tears. You should remember that their flowers cannot open their eyes in a cloudy sky. Our days are warm-hearted; if their coldness burns your face in the morning, their breeze will be amazing at night.

Here is our white boat, where our dreams chant their songs and our happy moments blossom. Its warm wood appeases my heart, and draws on my pulse a butterfly searching for your face. When you feel my shell in your hands and when you see my soul flying dreamily in front of your eyes, at that moment, you may remember our boat.

A Farmer's Chants

A Grey Tale

I know the wars and their ugly voices, because I am their son. War is a grey tale, dressing her red cloak in lonesome nights. It had stolen my blood and any smiling piece in me; so, you cannot see anything here but sad moments.

In the morning, our children fill their eyes with hazy clouds, and in the evening, you can smell the odor of hungry souls. The walls of our rooms are cracked like a smashed soul, and the beds of our brides are bloody like the colors of our streets. Youngsters and the elderly are sitting in dark corners waiting for their obscure fate, and every hand here has nothing but a paralysis. Without having committed a single sin, we are drowning in fiery fields, and you, the reader, do not do anything.

Anwer Ghani

Rocky Flowers

I remember my grandfather's flowers; they were silent and colorless like my life. They were always filled with fleeting blossoms, and incessantly hid themselves under grey veils. Those rocky flowers have dressed my face with its incomprehensible damages and with a womanly heart; they have colored my life with their bitter passion. They have taught me sadness since I saw my earth's tears, and as legendary heroes, they have filled my brooks with blood.

They are conquerors and have thousand songs, but I, the farmer from the south, know nothing about them. They are slender and bright, but their heart is rocky. When they visit our city, our Damask-rose disappears quickly, and our wells become bloody. There is no warmth in their hands and no place for my small dreams. There is nothing there but thorns uncovering their legs.

Believe me; all our sadness could not have happened without the silence of this soul which hides our dreams behind her absent head. It is here, in me, this icy tale which always kills my days in cold blood. She is not beautiful at all, and in one day, she shredded my kite fiercely. This murky soul teaches my flowers the war's songs, and slyly lies near our riverbank with her dark sorcery. She is a liar and blind like my moon.

A Farmer's Chants

Mirrors

Our trees which wear their wishes are just mirrors, swimming delightedly in distant seas. With blue chants, their shadows sit in the midst of the universe. I know as any bird does, my mirrors need a new open air, for the smoke of wars killed my wishes. I know as any young soldier does, dark souls cannot buy my Ambergris, and all the remnants of wars' voices are liars. We like the colors of flowers and the sounds of waterfalls. But what can I do if our mirrors were stolen in a blind night?

Their touches which descend in a dazzled evening cannot stay in my heart without scorching it. My eyes are too small to see the beautiful life that sits behind those mirrors. Please tell me: How can those mirrors wash my dream without any pain while my soul scours her destruction? I am a smashed shadow; so, do not try to see my face.

In the twilight, I try to kiss the faces of fairies, and in the evening, I drown delightedly in a hidden ocean. Now, you can see my shadowed soul sitting on the blue chair under her silky veil. She always attempts to catch the melodic colors and plant them in the ocean's mirrors.

Anwer Ghani

The Old Farmer

I am an old farmer, and lonely winds cannot find a place on my tongue. Like a green leaf, I cannot see my face but only in water, and all kisses of the North Mountains share my pillow with me. I love the sun when it burns my cheeks, and I madly love mud's smell because my father had planted me in our river. Yes, I am dissolving in our rivers as a young butterfly, and without any weariness, I shall repeat the birds' songs which give our blue flowers their free wings.

It is I, a farmer from the south where absurdity drowned in the gulf. My voice is a watery tale, and my yearning is an absent moment. One day, I had crossed into that sorcerous riverbank on a boat of silence. I had looked at the face of the field when it chanted its song. At that time, I had met the travelers' souls which gave me their treasures. They gifted my chest with unforgettable beats and hid their eternal secrets in my pockets.

I am a farmer who knows earth's scent. I grew between its pulses like a butterfly. Come, look at the sweetness of Euphrates! He does not know any spite. With a brown garment and a headband, he descended as a desert cavalier; so, it is not strange to see all that sand covering his face. I will also tell you about Uruk, the sleepy city of whose foundations were built by the seven wise men. Come, look at my palms and see how coarse they are, like our trees. You will find that darkness sits there, in that corner with its icy dress, killing my children.

A Farmer's Chants

The Bare Land

My life is salty like our grandfather's brook on whose sand we tried to plant trees in vain. Because of one angry moment, he had named it, "The Angry Stream – Azzalan". Because of its dead land, they had named its village, "The Bare Land – Alaria". Despite all the palms which he had planted around it, you cannot recognize its colorless face. I am not in the bare land, but its dry winds color my dreams.

Anwer Ghani

The Pained Land

All the moments of pain are just roads. They take my loneliness to a dark corner and teach it how to be recognizable. The pain is a cold story that dresses its colorful veil in the amazing twilight. No one can know the grey face of pain like the Iraqis. No one can recreate the brightness of eternal absence more perfectly than in my land. Yes, I am from here, the pained land. My father is the groaning, and my mother is the weeping.

A Farmer's Chants

Glamorous Gardens

The sun has two long braids, and goes out at dawn to her grandfather's flourishing orchard. It resembles the glamorous Kashmiri gardens, where faces are pure, reminding me of the ancestors, where white apples glimmer like pearls, wrapping themselves with silk.

They advised me to leave the purple coasts, because the truth is a free bird. They told me that Iraq is the brother of the sun. This was astonishing news to me. If so, where are the orchards of our beloved grandfathers? Where are the thriving gardens of Kashmir?

Anwer Ghani

Summer Is Not Beautiful

Our summer is not beautiful, because our girls have no new veils and our children have no smiles. In summer, the sea is windless and the sky is cloudless but the eyes of this world are blind to see my bare body. Summer is so inconsequential and my house is so summery that there is no sofa, no television and no life. Our morning is hot and empty, and our evening is dry and painful. Our summer is not beautiful because its sun is dark and its tales are sad.

A Farmer's Chants

Our Crazy Summer

I am from the south where the sun is naked and the rivers are waterless. I cannot give you a rose because our summer is a skilled flower-killer, and our butterflies retired on one anonymous day.

Our summer is crazy. His hair is uncombed and his radiance is strange. If you see his face, you will not forget his scowl, and if you touch his hand, you will not forget his coldness.

Our summer is crazy. He had taught us his inexplicable story that this world's people do not like our walking, always trying to push us from the bridge.

Anwer Ghani

The Faceless Land

We can smell all the scents of destruction because we are the sons of war. Its eyes kill our dreams and its hands slap our faces. When you walk in our land, you will tumble on our disposable souls, and in that dark corner, you will meet the faceless boys.

Yes, we are sons of war; our hands are empty and our souls are broken. Waterfalls cannot sooth our parched hearts, and rivers cannot revive our rocky roots.

There are no braids on our girls' heads because war has stolen everything here, every girl's braids. Their lips are scorched with deep cracks, and their faces are as colorless as our days. Here in Iraq, everything is empty – even the souls of girls. You will not see the childish jumps of their feet or the playful smiles of their arms. But you will see thin legs and a dried-out well.

I am from the faceless land where everything weeps – even the sun. Our women do not know anything else but cries. Their breasts have forgotten milk. They are the traces of wars; their mornings start with a wailing and their evenings end with a groan. Look at our trees! They are brassy and coarse like the voice of our women. Look at our lakes! They are dry like the riverbeds. There is no love here because the lips have retired. There is no beauty here because our women are faceless.

A Farmer's Chants

A Thirsty Bean

The sunset is a son of light, descending to the evening with azure eyes. He told me that the sun has long braids. He reminds me of the ancestors' apples. If only you saw them while they wrap themselves with silk . . .

Yes, in my crippled dream, I am ending as a thirsty bean. I am neither an almond tree nor a warm voice; so, I always bend in the morning with a snowy face and turn into a very cold tale.

As a thirsty bean, I have been looking for my face which was stolen by wars. I am the son of war; my heart is a dry desert, and my memory was kneaded by resilient dances. I am an Iraqi man; my life is postponed, and I know nothing about beauty or love. The cloth of my dreams is short, and all that I wish for is to see the waters of Euphrates without blood and for the shells to walk away from the crashed ribs of Babylon. All I what want is to live within the bean; the daughter of war. Just like I, it sleeps in the field without a face.

Anwer Ghani

The Dark Summer

Summer's kites are beautiful and bear our dreams on their wings, but our summer always cuts them and leaves us in tears.

Our summer is an old unsteady hazard, he knows nothing about our dry flowers. He sees our pain, but does not send any breeze to relieve our reddened cheeks.

Unlike our primitive souls, our summer is mysterious and dark. It has brought all the world's smolder into our land on one faceless night.

A Farmer's Chants

The River's Face

The river and the outlying flowers know the story. I do not tell them the secret of our southern treasure, but the bean has a loud voice, and you can hear all the news from her. She draws butterflies on our lips and makes a colorful breeze from our pain. She is warmhearted, and her pulse is always hot. From her face, the image of my soul emerges like a dazzled flower. She is blue and sleepy, and there is a white thorn on her left hand.

Anwer Ghani

Al-Mehdi

I see the deer and the wolf play together. Their souls are as lovely as the moon, and their hearts are delicate like a river. Women walk safely from Cairo to Baghdad over the flat grass and in a flowery aura. I look at the leader of justice; his eyes see the truth; his mouth is filled with knowledge and his heart is colored with mercifulness. He delights the hearts of his citizens with deep happiness, sates their souls with splendid wisdom and fills their hands with gold and diamonds. In that glorious moment, the sun is smooth like a veil, the moon is bright as a morning rose, and earth blushes like a bride.

When his country shines, the grass will smile, flowers will fly on wings, rivers will breathe out breezy love, and waterfalls will grin widely. Gold will color the earth, and diamonds will paint the trees. In that glory-filled moment, the Devil will have no voice, and the evil will have no aides.

When he appears, the trees will be loaded and flowers will be exceptionally amazing. He is the lover, the Sky man and the grandson of Abrahim. He is Al-Mahdi; his tongue does not know lying, and his hand does not slip. His name will be called by Gabriel, and his face will illuminate every heart. His fair words will push the Devil's deceit out of the souls, and his kindness will plant happiness in every house. Jesus will descend with him; so, the hearts of the West and the hands of the East will be one. Under the tent of God, the Earth will shine with Al-Mahdi's wisdom and Jesus' kindness. In that East-West land, everything will be colored with happiness, and souls will be completely freed from the voices of the evil.

A Farmer's Chants

The Arab River

I heard that the waters of rivers which breathe their laughs into wells will end in The Arab River. Birds which leave their eggs on high trees will build their nests in the garden of my grandfather. Clouds which overcast the sky will give their rain to our desert. The bombs which had been made in distant lands will sleep in my river's dreams. So, I am a legendary man, and my river is a kind heart.

Anwer Ghani

A River's Tales

The winter chants which our whispers composed had a delicate roar. At that time, the roads were wide because we were sons of old farmers who knew nothing about the river's tales. In fact, in "Al-Aria" – my childhood town, everything was simple, even the river-tales. You would not have had any reason to expect fairies in our water . . .

From that purity, we built primitive skyscrapers, just like our dreams. Now, you can imagine the smell of our feet; for, it had left unforgettable spells in our hearts. We did not know how our dirty feet could illuminate the darkness and whisper softly in the ears of our silence. We did not know the color of the sun at its beautiful sunset. That is to say . . . we are stolen people. At the same time, our trees had known everything. It is very strange that my tree knew everything, yet I do not know anything.

A Farmer's Chants

The Magical Wind

We are from the south where there are no leaves or flowers. Our ancestors had planted us in a bare land; so, the salty algae cover our souls.

There are no birds here in the south, and all that you can hear are the sound of delusional winds. They are not fairies, but I find every illusion in their palms. We love our magical winds because their white crowns sprinkle salty veils on our bare bodies so that we would not need more dreams.

You know, salty dreams can close up any door and bury any well. What I do not understand is how these illusional winds can play with our souls every single time . . .

Anwer Ghani

The Colorless City

Bears are not rough or brown, but rather soft like silky balloons, and the owl is not blind or ominous, but rather a witch whose pure heart can see the truth. They used to talk to me about the stories of my ancestors, but because of this cold city, rootlessness and homelessness, I have now decided to live in a warm nest on a tree to laugh as loudly as I can.

This city slapped me with her piercing hands and has stolen every beautiful thing from me. Because of it, I have forgotten my smile and my voice. A dumb man now is what I am, without color, exactly like this colorless city. I know nothing about the spring-deer and I cannot remember my dear trees. My soul is now in a big prison; the roads are smaller than my feet and the walls are taller than my dreams. This city has no mirror; so, you cannot see her face.

In that city, I find myself as a frozen picture on a wall. I am the son of green laughter. Look at me now: Do you see anything except drought? My land is dark, like the soul of this city, and the wail penetrating my breath is like the feet of the invaders. I lean on barefooted roads as an enigmatic story. There is nothing here but coldness. In my darkened street, I cannot see anything else but the stifling loss that tears my islands mercilessly. This is I: Just a heap of marginal fragments in a dark city that rides on me as if on a blind horse. I do not see anything else but stones gashing my feet, callous forms slashing my head, and hidden hands immersing me in muddy waters.

A Farmer's Chants

The Blind Wind

In a very strange moment, I saw the soul of a blind wind; it was shattered as our life in the south. That blind wind knew nothing but the destruction of my doors and bore nothing but deceptive seeds. Their colorful eyes are not attractive despite their velvety whispers. They fill my life with trembling limbs and paint my windows with cloudy tales.

The ignorant moon has no idea about her salty sorrows. When we talk about her wishes, we should understand the deep yearning which makes her heart jump over the grass like a rabbit. In fact, I did not see the tears of our blind wind, but my killed dream knows very well the colors of her moaning and the cooing of her eyes' dew. She sits at the western bank of our river like the sun, and she always narrates our ancestors' tales with a sad voice. Lastly, I have known from my mother that the salty taste of that wind had come from our sad stories.

Anwer Ghani

The Blind City

I am a blind tree that knows nothing about the evening breeze and its chants. All I know is a failing attempt to catch the ragged remnants of this world. My leaves are pale and my dream is a faint evening which sits before a black door without a sunset. The grey birds like its delusive whispers, but when it takes its real face, there is nothing but sad limbs.

I am from the blind city where nothing has eyes, even the girls. The bridges are so blind with weak breath, just like the eyelids of my sick bird.

In fact, our bridges have no eyes and they know nothing about our unique ways. When I touch their wood in the morning, I feel their pain, and when I hear their whispers at night, I see their sadness. Our blind bridges have an endless waste because their lost eyes are grey . . . like my soul.

A Farmer's Chants

Violet Tales

Our sun is violet but wears a white veil, and our trees are also sad but they unveil. Our tables are wide but empty, and our hearts are purple but broken. We are from the south where everything is violet, even our sons. When you immerse in our river, you will meet a violet fish, and when you read my poem, you will discover all the violet tales. Here, the violet rose knows how to hug the fabled river in a moment when it needs a warm touch.

I will drown in yearning; I will find that train where we meet our story. She told me that the moon sleeps on free eyelids, and when you know a red kiss, you will see the cloud-flowers.

Anwer Ghani

Nothing in My Soul but Loss

The windows are important because my father had said that winds are always kissing the glasses of the windows in the early morning. I can see the souls of the winds, but the problem is situating in my fingers where all the stories of absence reside. In fact, I am trying to color my soul with a windy gaze, but as you see, there is nothing else here in my soul but loss.

My years are affectionate because all the trees which we had seen in a special moment are absent. I like the absent moment and I love the absent fragrance of my grandfather. The colors are the remainders of a love story, and my eye is an old lover. Now, sit please, and do not worry! I am alright; I am not crazy; I just try to live without my lost love.

I am a lean tree branch of a magical dawn; there is no sun on my forehead and no kiss on my neck. I know the freedom very well, but I cannot see the road.

Yes, I am a blind bird, and I should learn from the freedom's kiss how to see life. There, on the mouths of freedom-shapers, you will find those violet kisses.

A Farmer's Chants

Dreamy Butterflies

Our women's wishes are filled with pink dreams, and their desires dissolve in hidden windows on secret nights. Here on the colorful limbs, you can see nothing but arousing smiles and inspiring whispers. The hearts are fragile, but they can see your brightness and hear your chants. There are no wings here, but rather dreamy butterflies which know nothing but love.

Yes, there are dreamy butterflies, carrying windy stories in their hearts and matutinal breezes in their palms.

Anwer Ghani

Blind Hotels

Streets, cafes and markets are human. Dresses, perfumes and bags are human. Trees, waterfalls and flowers are human. The snow, sands and salt are human. Yet, in spite of all these human things, our spiritual hotels are empty.

Our hotel is small and dark despite its large gardens. In our hotel, the walls are thick and souls are discordant. We are good at making walls, and someday, we may see strangers here buying walls from us. Our walls are perfect and unbelievable; they prevent any love or any warm hands.

There are no stairs in our small hotel because we are crippled. When he whispered to me, I saw the sofa steal his coat, but you know I could not say anything because of the blood on it.

I think you can imagine now the size of the windows in our small hotel. Yes, they are smaller than my eyes, and because of that, the people call our hotel "The Blind Hotel".

A Farmer's Chants

Crying

There is no waterfall in Iraq, and all that I can see is the hostile desert. Our dresses are black, and our women are shadows of cries. I am a man without form. Like birds, my home is a simple nest under the merciless sun. Look at my skin! It is dry. Look at my eyes! They are misleading. My morning is a painful story, and my evening is a sad memory. There is nothing here but the crying. Yes, in Iraq, everything is destroyed, even beautiful women.

Anwer Ghani

Grey Butterflies

The silence is the journey of my sleepy soul. It does not know anything but whispers. Look at it! It stands there like a desert-bird where salty sands color its face. Its yellow fragrance fills our shadowed dreams. Look at my hidden places; they migrate toward remote wells where the butterflies of the grey silence narrate my wild stillness.

A Farmer's Chants

Spring's Lover

Spring sparkles like a girl, and when its water wakes up, it mixes its coffee with all the blue songs. I am spring's lover, and in yearning moments, I cannot hide my passion. What can I do if my soul's windows cannot see anything else but the charming breeze?

Anwer Ghani

I Love Writers

I love writers because my mother said that they descend from a magical paradise and that hidden demons live in their souls. The legend says that the writers awake early to seize dreams and they knock on snow's doors before white dogs to tell us winter's stories. The snowy mountains are deeply in love with the warm cloaks of writers and the flying horses that emerge from their fingers, changing the gloomy colors. I have seen the souls of writers jump delightedly over the grass with deer and birds taking their chants from their silver-tongued pens. You may feel the soft breeze playing with their eyes, and you may sense their fervent strokes when they disappear in the river's smiles.

A Farmer's Chants

A Bloody Lake

My friend told me that there is a beautiful lake near his home. At that moment, I remembered our lake.

Yes, in Iraq there is a lake, but it has been filled with blood. It has piercing eyes, and her voice is sad like my heart. When I see it, I remember our bare children and all the weeping mothers. Yes, we live in a sad land where you cannot find any dream . . . just a bloody lake.

Anwer Ghani

A Bitter Soul

My grandfather once said: there is nothing like a cold brook where the watery breeze has colored the silky butterflies. I am a man from the south where streams cover our fields, but I cannot remember any one of them. My grandfather was a farmer from the south, and he connected its brooks. He was keeping the tales of the green land in his chest as a treasure, but his grandson knows nothing about the southern tales and sees nothing but a dry life. So, you are seeing my bitter soul and you are feeling my thirsty heart.

A Farmer's Chants

He Who Saw Light

I love the mud because it was a memory of your great hands. I feel proud when I see the flights of those who arrive at your door and sit there, seeking nectar from your big secrets.

Yes, I know, you look at us – the primitive – with a smile because you are Sin Liqui who saw everything. Here, we are talking about infinity, but you had kneaded it between your fingers and illuminated its dark cities with abundant light. I see you on the brassy Uruk-porches looking at us with a cup of tea-glitters like a Babylonian angel who plays in the wilderness with Enkidu's deer.

Yes, your hands defeated the aging and death because you saw the secrets. O, Sin Liqui Unninni, you look at us and smile, because you saw the light! When you found a sound, your journey became a river, and when you wrapped the light, my soul became a flower, and when you met the sun, I found hope. I am a flower from sand's cities who suffers from love like a shepherd who had been drowning in the gulf. I am standing in that corner, enumerating yearning's breaths. In one day, I had bravely crossed the silence on a boat of light. I had looked at the faces of fields when they were chanting their lovely songs. In that moment, light's souls held my hand and gifted me their precious treasure. They blazed my ribs with an unforgotten flutter and stroked my head with fiery stones.

Anwer Ghani

A Pale Man

Our sky has inherited the worry-clouds from the grey ancestors. It was waiting for migrant holidays; however, our souls had nothing but gloomy faces. Our sky is a tear of a crying land where sad rivers had written their stories. Here, you cannot see anything else but dry flowers, and in our hidden corners, you will find a pale moon with a rough face. Look at me! I am the son of the pale moon. My hand is very cold and my lips are ripped like a widow's heart.

I am a man made from wood, and I do not know anything about lying. I do not like these pale lights which lying voices brought to my town. May I stand in the heart of this waterfall? I mean . . . away from your pale lightness?

I am a lifeless tree with colorless tales. I am a pale man who cannot live on a fearless boat. Here in my destroyed land, there is no glory nor poems, and all that you can see is a pale death. Our houses are filled with black bitterness and our grass is not green. Our girls are fields of sadness, and our streets are mirrors of wars. Yes, we are the sons of a blind death, but there are no stains on our hands and no blood of others on our coats.

A Farmer's Chants

The Grey Bird

I have a salty bird who had not tried to fly because he has no wings since his birth. His color was grey in the black era because of faked praise. I am not a revolutionary man, and I always try to walk beside the wall, but my bird has a passionate soul, and he has quickly changed his color to hold any remains.

Anwer Ghani

The Silent Tree

These birds love the silent tree and like to perch on that limb. You know, love is an unexplained thing, but we know it very well. From that lovely branch, leaves and feathers had fallen with a quarrelsome smile. This was a heavy thing for that tired tree which is filled with sad stories. She always descends to clean the ground from the frivolous feathers. Her slim fingers drown butterflies, and her broken heart chants absent songs. I saw her kiss water – like my voice, which I had forgotten at my postponed beginning.

I am a wild man who knows the animals' sounds but is not pure like they are. Bears are neither rough nor brown, and the owl is silver and sees the truth. I was smiling at that glory in the morning, and for many times I was sitting at a lake. I did not remember its name. I am rootless now; my small hut had lost its threads, and my cloak had been colored with forgetfulness. This angry city had slapped me mercilessly and immersed oblivion in my memory. I have been crying bitterly since that time where I had seen her. I am crying for my precious trees. I had forgotten my color and my voice. I am very sad and colorless now and never remember the smiles of my missing trees.

I am a yellow tree with cold whispers. As a thirsty thorn, I am waiting for crippled dreams. My streets had been stolen and my brooks know nothing but pallor. In April, children fly lovely kites while my birds disappear in the mud with motionless souls.

Oh, my days, here is a wound, please listen to it!

A Farmer's Chants

The Glorious Friday

I love that fragrance which I knew very well and felt on that glorious Friday in that luminous corner of the sky. I love his words when he says, "this is the respectable Al-Mehdi who will fill the towns with wisdom." I see his turban with its uncurled end and see his horse; it is flawless and aglow like a gem. The lands will recognize his forgivingness, touch his mercifulness and smell his Vestal essence. Jesus will descend with him to show the globe the shining dawn and guide souls to truth. His sword is resolute but merciful, and his words are forceful but just.

Anwer Ghani

Illusions

My smile does not eat her breakfast and my eyes become brilliant because of their illusions. Now, I can see a faint light with a silver skin like the moon. I see a brave one's ship swimming under my destroyed roof, traveling through infinity as a shadow. It is flying in my broad illusions as a bird. Yes, I am here, with this motionless brain and useless body, an eastern man drowning in the illusions.

I am a physician, and I know very well the burning taste of the strange moments of illusion. They are like the grey papers which had disappeared in salty seas without pain. Because of the hidden voice of that watching soul, all that I can see are our dry leaves which have colored our empty eyes. You should know now that I am in thirsty times and my heart is faint like a dry illusion.

In fact, I find the pleasure to color the sun's eyelashes with magical dreams. I like coffee because my skin is brown, and coffee brings the images of my ancestors back to me. Yes, my brown skin is made from the coffee-illusion, but my heart is a city of sadness. Here in Iraq, birds are made from illusions and trees are just stories of tears.

Actually, no . . . there are no birds in Iraq, and what I have talked about is just an illusion because of our sorcerous coffee.

A Farmer's Chants

The Cloud-Tales

It is silvery – just like my dream, this winter which I began to feel intensely. His rain colors my soul and plants in me unforgettable tales.

When I learned its laughs, the moonlight slept in my lids, and when I touched the face of a distant voice, the glow of magical instruments colored my dark nights. With all its glory, the cloud showed me its heart and planted its tales deeply in my soul. I feel them deeply, and I remember their scent very well. How can you possibly imagine them? How can you count the cloud-tales?

Do you hear its tale? She touches my heart with a whisper from a far-off love. All of the velvety days take their colors from her water, and our tender land drowns in her tales with untold smiles. Her dreams fill our spirits with freedom's breaths, and on her hands, you can see a beautiful paint. Our hearts, however, are too young to understand her glances.

Anwer Ghani

A Remote Scent

She showed me the soul of pink flowers and the hidden colors of life. So, the angels who know everything add nothing, and the sorcerers who do everything do nothing. The world takes his meaning from her essence, and candles have no souls in the absence of her gentle touch. You cannot feel the days' pulses without her scent and the riverbanks' flowers cannot find their chants anywhere else but in her eyes. In fact, I cannot continue to live in the desert because my horses sense her remote scent. This remote scent has reached me in the last days when I was driving my thought toward surrealistic freemen. Believe me, I know that it has inspirational windows, and its sky has awesome colors. But what can I do, if all my doors were stolen and all my eyes were closed by the unknown?

… epilogue

about the Author

Anwer Ghani is an Iraqi award-winning poet. He was born in 1973 in Hilla. A consultant nephrologist and a religious scholar, he has authored more than seventy books – most of them in Arabic, with eleven in English. His name has appeared in more than thirty literary journals and ten anthologies in the USA and the UK.

In 2017, the India branch of Stratford University rewarded the author with an Achievement Certificate. In the same year, he was nominated by the World Nations Writers Union as world's best poet, and was distinguished for his globe-reaching poetry with the Rock Pebbles Award in 2019.

Anwer Ghani's poetry signifies itself through realistic imagination and an imaginary narrative, and centers around the sadness of war and the glorification of simple life.

Inner Child Press

Inner Child Press is a publishing company founded and operated by writers. Our personal publishing experiences provide us an intimate understanding of the sometimes-daunting challenges writers, new and seasoned may face in the business of publishing and marketing their creative "Written Work".

For more information

Inner Child Press

www.innerchildpress.com

intouch@innerchildpress.com

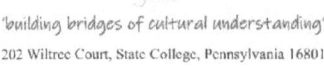

'building bridges of cultural understanding'
202 Wiltree Court, State College, Pennsylvania 16801

www.innerchildpress.com

www.ingramcontent.com/pod-product-compliance
Lightning Source LLC
Chambersburg PA
CBHW032019040426
42448CB00006B/664